W9-CQJ-766

Fact Finders®

Biographies

Louis Armstrong
Jazz Legend

by Elizabeth Raum

Consultant:
Dan Morgenstern, Director
Institute of Jazz Studies
Rutgers University
Newark, New Jersey

Capstone *press*®

Mankato, Minnesota

Fact Finders is published by Capstone Press,
151 Good Counsel Drive, P.O. Box 669, Mankato, Minnesota 56002.
www.capstonepress.com

Library of Congress Cataloging-in-Publication Data
Raum, Elizabeth.
    Louis Armstrong : jazz legend / by Elizabeth Raum.
    p. cm.—(Fact finders. Biographies. Great African Americans)
    Includes bibliographical references and index.
    ISBN-13: 978-0-7368-6419-0 (hardcover)
    ISBN-10: 0-7368-6419-9 (hardcover)
    1. Armstrong, Louis, 1901–1971—Juvenile literature. 2. Jazz musicians—United
States—Biography—Juvenile literature. 3. African American jazz musicians—Biography—
Juvenile literature. I. Title. II. Series.
ML3930.A75R37 2007
781.65092—dc22   2005037565

Summary: An introduction to the life of Louis Armstrong, the musician and singer who
    helped popularize jazz throughout the world.

Editorial Credits
John Bliss and Jennifer Murtoff (Navta Associates), editors; Juliette Peters, set designer;
    Jan Calek (Navta Associates), book designer; Wanda Winch, photo researcher/
    photo editor

Photo Credits
Capstone Press Archives, 26 (bottom); Corbis, 19; Corbis/Bettmann, 23, 25; Corbis/Philip
Gould, 11; Corbis/Profiles in History, 1; Courtesy of the Louis Armstrong House &
Archives, 15, 22; Courtesy of the Louisiana State Museum, 9, 16; Frank Driggs Collection,
18; Getty Images Inc./Frank Driggs Collection, 7, 13, 17; Getty Images Inc./Hulton Archive,
cover, 27; Getty Images Inc./Hulton Archive/Haywood Magee, 5; Getty Images Inc./
Hulton Archive/P. L. Sperr, 8; Getty Images Inc./Keystone, 26 (top); Getty Images Inc./
Time Life Pictures/Time Magazine, Copyright Time Inc., 21

1 2 3 4 5 6 11 10 09 08 07 06

Table of Contents

Chapter 1

Scat

"Rip-bip-ee-doo-dee-doot, doo . . . "

Louis Armstrong's deep, **gravelly** voice surprised the control booth crew at a recording session in Chicago in 1926. Armstrong had been singing real words. Then he switched to **scat**, singing like a **jazz** instrument.

Combining the words of scat with jazz music was a new idea. Many people believed that Armstrong invented scat. He didn't. But when he combined scat singing with jazz music, Armstrong changed American music forever. He taught singers how to use their voices like musical instruments. Armstrong used both his voice and his instrument to express sadness and joy.

FACT!

African American musicians in New Orleans began playing a new kind of music around 1900. This music combined blues, ragtime, marches, gospel songs, and spirituals. It later became known as jazz.

Louis Armstrong reacts with joy during a jazz concert.

Chapter 2

Beginnings

Even as a child, Louis Armstrong was creative and hardworking. He had to be. He was born on August 4, 1901, in a poor neighborhood in New Orleans, Louisiana. His father, Willie, left soon after Armstrong was born. His mother, Mary Ann, was only a teenager. She worked hard, but the family never had enough money. Armstrong did what he could to help his mother and his younger sister, Beatrice. He loved them with all his heart.

FACT!

Mary Ann always called her son Louis. It was the name he liked best. His friends called him Dipper or Dippermouth because of his great big grin. Later, Armstrong wrote a song called "Dippermouth Blues."

This picture of Louis, Mary Ann, and Beatrice Armstrong was taken in 1922 when Armstrong was 21 years old.

7

First Horn

When Armstrong was only seven, he began working for the Karnofskys, a Russian Jewish family in the neighborhood. He rode on their junk wagon and blew a big tin horn. The horn reminded people to bring out their bottles, rags, or whatever they wanted to sell. Even though the horn was only a noisemaker, Armstrong found a way to cup his hands around the mouthpiece and play simple tunes.

Armstrong grew up in New Orleans, shown here in 1915. ▼

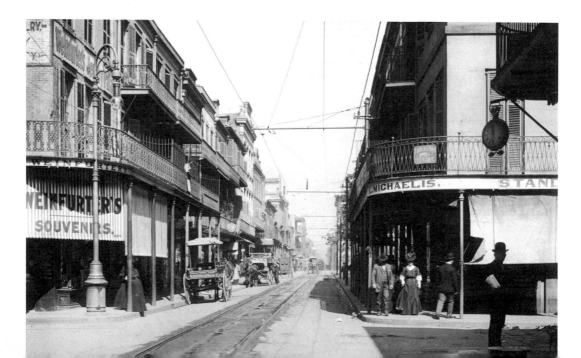

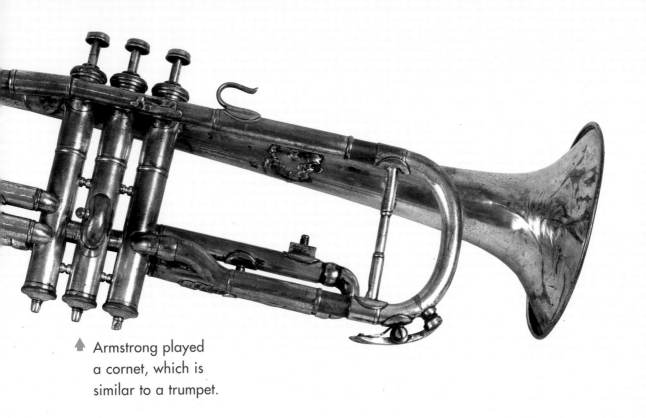

▲ Armstrong played a cornet, which is similar to a trumpet.

One day when he was 11, Armstrong saw a brass **cornet** in the window of a **pawnshop**. The Karnofskys lent him the money that he needed to buy it. He paid back every penny.

QUOTE

When Armstrong grew up, he said, "when I reached the age of 11, I began to realize it was the Jewish family who instilled in me singing from the heart."

Brass Bands

Armstrong was surrounded by music. He followed the brass bands leading funeral parades. He listened to musicians playing on the sidewalk in front of the Funky Butt Hall, a club near his house on Perdido Street. He met Joseph "King" Oliver, the best cornet player in town. Sometimes he let Armstrong carry his horn. Armstrong wanted to be a musician like King Oliver.

Armstrong worked long hours to help his mother. He missed many days of school. After fifth grade, he left school. Armstrong and his friends Little Mac, Redhead, Happy Bolton, and Big Nose Sidney sang and danced on street corners for pennies.

Armstrong liked to listen to brass bands playing funeral parades, a tradition that continues today.

On New Year's Eve, when Armstrong was 12, he got into serious trouble. People in New Orleans celebrated the New Year by shooting off firecrackers or firing guns into the air. Armstrong took a gun that belonged to his mother's boyfriend and shot it into the air. A police officer arrested Armstrong and took him to jail.

After a night in jail, Armstrong went to court. The judge was worried that if the boy remained at home, he would continue to get into trouble. The judge sent Armstrong to the Colored Waif's Home, a **reformatory** for boys who had gotten into trouble. It was run by a caring African American man named Captain Joseph Jones. The reformatory turned out to be a good thing for Louis Armstrong and a good thing for American music.

First Band

The Colored Waif's Home had a band. Armstrong begged to be allowed to join. Once he proved he could behave, the band director agreed. He gave Armstrong a tambourine, then a snare drum, a bugle, and finally a cornet.

QUOTE

"My whole success goes back to the time I was arrested as a wayward boy of 12 . . . I began to learn music."
—Louis Armstrong

Armstrong played with the Colored Waif's Home Brass Band. He is in the middle of the top row, with his hand on his leg. ▼

Armstrong learned quickly. He led the band in parades. When Armstrong led the band along Perdido Street, all his old neighbors cheered. So did his mother, which made Armstrong happy.

Chapter 4

Success

In 1915, when Armstrong was 14, he left the Colored Waif's Home. He worked odd jobs as a laborer. This didn't stop Armstrong from playing cornet all night in local clubs. He barely slept. He dreamed of becoming a full-time musician.

Soon, Armstrong's idol, King Oliver, left for Chicago to lead a jazz band. He suggested that Armstrong take his place in the Kid Ory Band. Armstrong, who was 15, loved playing with Ory. On his first night, Armstrong's eyes lit up and he broke into a big grin. Then he blew his horn so loudly that he drowned out the band. Armstrong learned to play more softly, but he never stopped smiling.

"There were many good, experienced trumpet players in town, but none of them had young Louis's possibilities."
—Kid Ory

Armstrong smiles as he poses with his horn. He followed King Oliver to Chicago in 1922, a few years before this picture was taken.

In 1918, Armstrong married Daisy Parker. His mother wished them well, but the Armstrongs had a troubled marriage. They divorced in 1923.

Armstrong and the band in which he played on the riverboat *S.S. Capitol*. Armstrong is third from right.

During this time, Armstrong played cornet on the riverboats that traveled up and down the Mississippi River. People all along the river heard the sweet sound of his horn. When the riverboat docked, crowds came on board to dance to the band.

Moving North

King Oliver's Creole Jazz Band was a hit in Chicago. In 1922, when Oliver decided to add another cornet to the band, he sent for Armstrong. Armstrong packed his cornet and put on his best suit. Because his mother had heard it was cold in Chicago, she made him wear long underwear.

Armstrong was happy in King Oliver's band. Both Armstrong and Oliver played cornet. When they played together, it was as if those horns were talking to each other.

In 1922, Armstrong (center, foreground) joined King Oliver's Creole Jazz Band in Chicago. He sometimes played the slide trumpet.

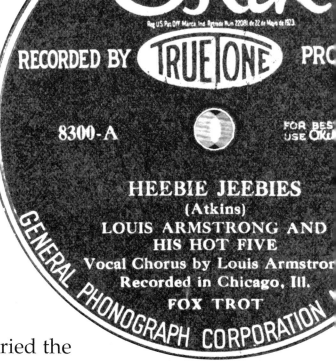

Recording

In 1924, Armstrong married the band's piano player, Lil Hardin. His new wife suggested that Armstrong go to New York City to play with the Fletcher Henderson Orchestra. He took her advice.

His playing impressed both New York audiences and musicians. Duke Ellington, who later became a great bandleader, brought his band to the Roseland Ballroom to hear Armstrong play. Armstrong was a genius. He influenced trumpet players and musicians of all kinds, but nobody could play quite like he did.

Louis Armstrong's Hot Five, Exclusive Okeh Record

Armstrong made a famous recording of scat, "Heebie Jeebies," with his Hot Five band.

When he returned to Chicago in 1925, Armstrong began making records with his own band. He mixed the old-time music of New Orleans with **improvised solos,** which let band members express their own musical ideas. Between 1925 and 1928, Armstrong and his bands recorded more than 60 songs. One song, "Heebie Jeebies," is the first popular recording of scat singing.

Chapter 5

Fame

In 1932, a year after separating from Lil, Armstrong went to Europe for the first time. Armstrong lived in Europe during 1934. A writer in England gave him a new nickname: Satchmo. The name was a shortened form of *satchel*, a type of suitcase, and *mouth*. People everywhere began to call Armstrong "Satchmo."

Armstrong returned to the United States in 1935. He toured with his band, made records, and appeared in movies. He made more movies than any other jazz musician. In 1937, he had his own radio show. Armstrong was a star.

In 1938, he married Alpha Smith. It was his third marriage, but not his last.

TIME

THE WEEKLY NEWSMAGAZINE

Artzybasheff

LOUIS ARMSTRONG
When you got to ask what it is, you never get to know.
(Music)

Armstrong quickly became famous and was featured in magazines, movies, and radio shows.

QUOTE

"When Lucille came along, I knew she was it, the right one."
—Louis Armstrong

Lucille

In 1942, Armstrong finally met his true love, Lucille Wilson. Their marriage lasted 29 years. They bought a home in Queens, New York. Armstrong never had children of his own. But he loved them and spent hours with the kids in his neighborhood.

The Armstrongs visited many countries with his band. Presidents and kings cheered Louis Armstrong. His great big smile, his gravelly voice, and his amazing horn captured the hearts of people young and old, rich and poor, at home and away.

▲ Armstrong loved children and enjoyed spending time with them.

Armstrong's performances, including a stop in Ghana (above), drew huge crowds.

Huge crowds gathered wherever Armstrong played. In Ghana, Africa, 100,000 people came to hear Armstrong perform. In the European country of Hungary, 93,000 people attended his concert in a Budapest soccer stadium.

Chapter 6

Final Notes

In 1964, Armstrong recorded the title song from the Broadway musical *Hello, Dolly!* It became a number one hit. The musical *Hello, Dolly!* was made into a movie in 1969, and Armstrong sang the song with Barbra Streisand. This was his last movie.

Armstrong had a heart attack in 1969. His last job playing was at the Waldorf-Astoria in February of 1971. In March, he had a second heart attack. He died peacefully in his sleep on July 6, 1971.

QUOTE

"They all know I'm here in the cause of happiness . . . Through all of the misfortunes, etc., I did not plan anything. Life was there for me and I accepted it. And life, whatever came out, has been beautiful to me, and I love everybody."

—Louis Armstrong

Armstrong smiles outside of the Academy Awards theater in 1968. He sang "The Bare Necessities" as part of the evening's festivities.

Armstrong's funeral was held near his home in Queens, New York.

Over 25,000 people waited in line to pay their last respects to Louis Armstrong. A few days later, New Orleans held a jazz funeral. Thousands watched as brass bands wound through the streets of New Orleans.

Legacy

Armstrong's music lives on. He still brings joy and laughter to people as they listen to and watch recordings of him and his music. Musicians still try to play like Armstrong did. Singers try to copy his style. But Louis Armstrong was one of a kind, an American legend.

In 1995, the United States Postal Service issued a Louis Armstrong stamp.

Fast Facts

Full name: Louis Daniel Armstrong

Nicknames: Little Louis, Dippermouth, Pops, Satchelmouth, Satchmo

Birth: August 4, 1901

Death: July 6, 1971

Parents: William and Mary Ann (called Mayann) Armstrong

Sister: Beatrice (called Mama Lucy)

Hometown: New Orleans, Louisiana

Wives: Daisy Parker (1918–1922), Lil Hardin (1924–1932), Alpha Smith (1938–1942), Lucille Wilson (1942–1971)

Achievements:

One of the first people to record scat singing

Introduced extended instrumental solo to jazz

First African American performer sponsored on national radio broadcasts

One of the first African Americans showcased in major Hollywood movies

Recorded thousands of songs over five decades

Time Line

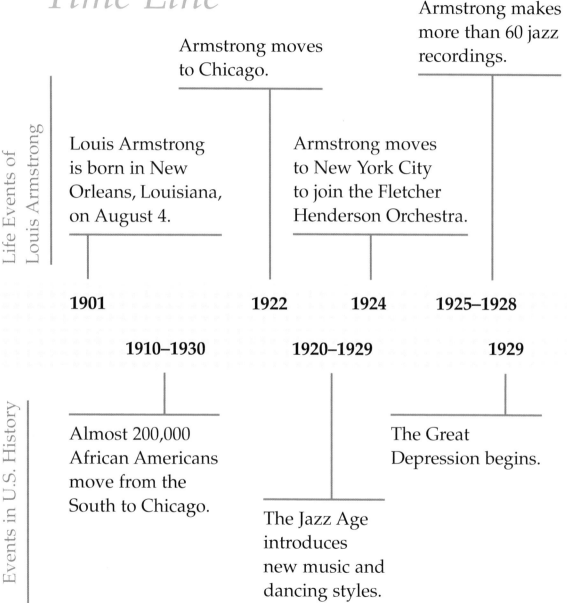

Life Events of Louis Armstrong

Armstrong moves to Chicago.

Armstrong makes more than 60 jazz recordings.

Louis Armstrong is born in New Orleans, Louisiana, on August 4.

Armstrong moves to New York City to join the Fletcher Henderson Orchestra.

1901   **1922**   **1924**   **1925–1928**

1910–1930   **1920–1929**   **1929**

Events in U.S. History

Almost 200,000 African Americans move from the South to Chicago.

The Great Depression begins.

The Jazz Age introduces new music and dancing styles.

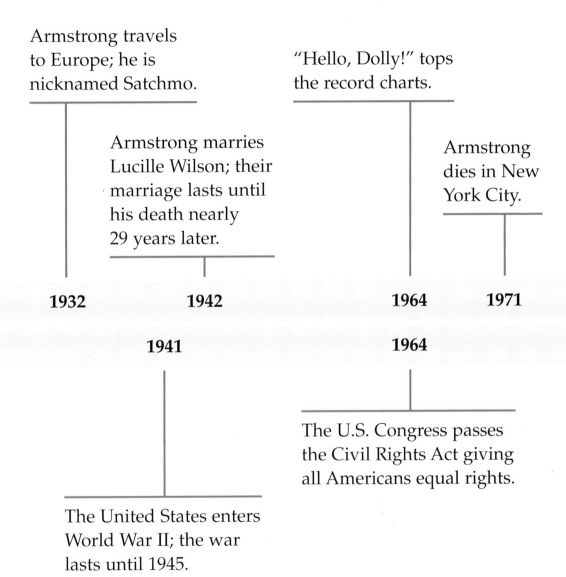

Armstrong travels to Europe; he is nicknamed Satchmo.

"Hello, Dolly!" tops the record charts.

Armstrong marries Lucille Wilson; their marriage lasts until his death nearly 29 years later.

Armstrong dies in New York City.

1932   **1942**   **1964**   **1971**

1941   **1964**

The U.S. Congress passes the Civil Rights Act giving all Americans equal rights.

The United States enters World War II; the war lasts until 1945.

Glossary

cornet (kor-NET)—a brass musical instrument that is similar to but shorter than a trumpet

gravelly (GRAV-uh-lee)—having a rough or grating sound

improvised (IM-pruh-vized)—made up on the spot

jazz (JAZ)—a lively, rhythmical type of music in which players often make up their own tunes and add new notes in unexpected places

pawnshop (PAWN-shop)—a shop where people can leave a valuable item in return for a loan; the item is returned if the loan is paid back, otherwise items are sold to other customers.

reformatory (ri-FOR-muh-tor-ee)—a special school or institution for young people who have broken the law

scat (SKAT)—jazz singing with nonsense syllables

solo (SOH-loh)—a piece of music that is played or sung by one person, with or without accompaniment

Internet Sites

FactHound offers a safe, fun way to find Internet sites related to this book. All of the sites on FactHound have been researched by our staff.

Here's how:

1. Visit *www.facthound.com*

2. Choose your grade level.

3. Type in this book ID **0736864199** for age-appropriate sites. You may also browse subjects by clicking on letters, or by clicking on pictures and words.

4. Click on the **Fetch It** button.

FactHound will fetch the best sites for you!

Read More

Elish, Dan. *Louis Armstrong and the Jazz Age.* Cornerstones of Freedom. New York: Children's Press, 2005.

Fahlenkamp-Merrell, Kindle. *Louis Armstrong.* Journey to Freedom. Chanhassen, Minn.: Child's World, 2002.

Kimmel, Eric. *A Horn for Louis.* A Stepping Stone Book. New York: Random House, 2005.

Index